D1706923

Why Is It Hot?

A **Just Ask**™ Book

by Chris Arvetis
and Carole Palmer

illustrated by
Vernon McKissack

FIELD PUBLICATIONS
MIDDLETOWN, CT.

It is so hot.
I've never felt this hot.
Why is it so hot?

It is very hot!

That's a good question.

I sure can.
When we talk about how hot
it is, we are talking about
the weather.
To learn about the weather
we can study temperature,
wind, and water.

Temperature,
wind, and
water.

First, let's find out about
the temperature.
Look at the earth.
The X shows where we are.
At this time of the year
our part of the earth is
tilted toward the sun.

SUN

EARTH

The sun shines brightly
on the earth.
It heats up the air and land.
The temperature goes higher
and higher.
AND IT IS HOT!

We use a thermometer to find out what the temperature is.
Look at the thermometer.
The red line is at 90.
The bigger the number, the hotter it is.

Next, let's look at my weather map.

The yellow band shows the part of the world that is hot all the time.

Warm, dry air starts over the land.

Warm, moist air begins over the water.

EUROPE

NORTH AMERICA

AFRICA

EQUATOR

SOUTH AMERICA

We also need to know
about the wind.

Wind is moving air.

The arrows show the
direction the air moves.

When the cooler air mixes
with the warm moist air,
we get rain.

NORTH
AMERICA

SO
AME

EQUATOR

The amount of water in the air also makes us feel hot.

On a rainy day, we can see the water in the air.

We can see the raindrops.

Today, there is another kind of water in the air.

We cannot see it, but we can feel it.

It makes the air feel wet.

We call it HUMIDITY.

A lot of humidity in the air
makes us feel hot and sticky.
We get little bubbles
of water on our skin.

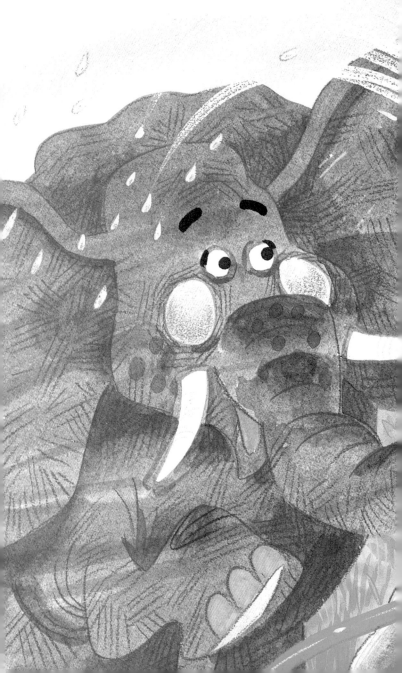

I've noticed that!

On a humid day, the water
just sits on our skin.
It makes us feel hotter
and hotter.

NORTH
AMERICA

SOUTH
AMERICA

Let's review—
The yellow band shows where
the warm air started.
This air moved toward us.
The arrows show the
route it took.

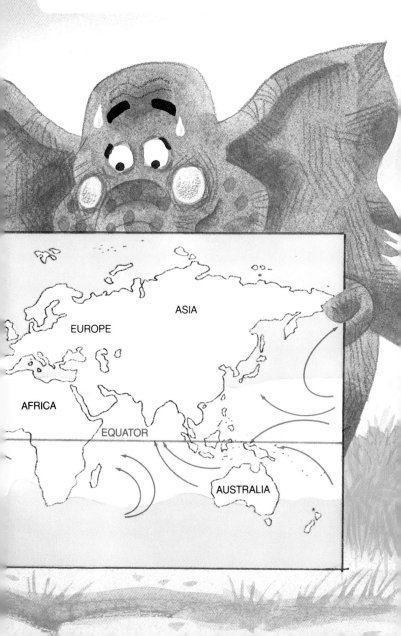

The humidity makes us feel hot and sticky.

We're thirsty!

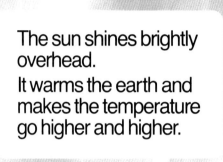

The sun shines brightly
overhead.
It warms the earth and
makes the temperature
go higher and higher.